Learn Sp   Week

CHRISTINA TORRES

All rights Reserved. No part of this publication or the information in it may be quoted from or reproduced in any form by means such as printing, scanning, photocopying or otherwise without prior written permission of the copyright holder.

Disclaimer and Terms of Use: Effort has been made to ensure that the information in this book is accurate and complete, however, the author and the publisher do not warrant the accuracy of the information, text and graphics contained within the book due to the rapidly changing nature of science, research, known and unknown facts and the Internet. The Author and the publisher do not hold any responsibility for errors, omissions or contrary interpretation of the subject matter herein. This book is presented solely for motivational and informational purposes only.

Contents

Thank You and a Free Gift 1

Introduction 2

Lesson 1 Letters and Their Sounds 3

   Pronouncing the letters 3

   Alphabet and letter names 6

   Accents 9

Lesson 2 Greetings and Basic Expressions 11

Lesson 3 Numbers, Months, Days and Time 17

   The numbers 17

   Dates 19

      Months 19

      Days 20

      Age and Birthdays 22

   Time 24

      Ordinal Numbers 25

Lesson 4 Nouns: Genders and Plurals 27

   Gender 27

      Feminine Nouns 28

      Masculine Nouns 30

Neutral Nouns 31

Plural 33

Free Course – Speak in a Week! 36

Lesson 5 Articles and Pronouns 37

Articles 37

Pronouns 39

Subject Pronouns 40

Possesive Pronouns 42

Demonstratives 43

Lesson 6 Adjectives 44

Neuter adjectives 2

Regular adjectives 2

Descriptive Adjectives 48

Colors 53

Nationalities 54

Lesson 7 Prepositions and Seasons 56

Prepositions 56

Seasons 59

Lesson 8 Verbs in the Present Tense 60

"Ar" verbs 61

"Er" verbs 64

"Ir" verbs 67

Summary 70

Additional Resources for Further Study 71

Thank You and a Free Gift

As a way of saying thanks for reading this book, I want to share three videos with you that have revolutionized the way people learn new languages. These short, but powerful, videos reveal the latest secrets, tips, and tricks that can greatly reduce the time it takes you to read, write, and speak in a new language.

Visit http://www.deepthoughtpress.com/languages to watch them now.

Thanks and let's get started!

Christina

Introduction

Welcome to the amazing experience of learning Spanish. This book will help you learn Spanish with easy and short lessons. This method is super simple and I wish it had been available when I first started learning Spanish because it would have saved me months of studying. You are about to start learning one of the most romantic languages in the world and although this can be a bit challenging, do not become discouraged! You certainly can do this!

Lesson 1 Letters and Their Sounds

Pronouncing the letters

Reading and pronouncing written Spanish is much simpler than doing the same in English. This is because most letters represent one single sound, and those which don't have very clear rules to follow. Check out the table below. You will see each letter and an example for an approximate pronunciation in English.

LETTER	PRONUNCIATION
A	Like *a* in *rap*
B	Like *b* in *bat*

C	Like *c* in *century* when it's placed before vowels e and i
	Like *ch* in *champion* when it's placed before h
	Like *c* in *cat* when it's placed anywhere else
D	Like *d* in *do*
E	Like *e* in *bed*
F	Like *f* in *food*
G	Like *h* in *have* when it's placed before the vowels e and i
	Like *g* in *gap* when it's placed anywhere else
H	Silent
I	Like *i* in *big*
J	Like *h* in *her*
K	Like *k* in *key*
L	Like *l* in *long*
	Like *j* in *jean* when it's placed before another L
M	Like *m* in *mom*
N	Like *n* in *no*
Ñ	Like *ny* in *canyon*

O	Like *o* in *hop*
P	Like *p* in *pet*
Q	Like *q* in *quote*. It's always followed by a *u* which is silent when it's placed before e and i
R	Similar to *r* in *ring* when it's placed before another r or at the beginning of a word. This pronunciation does not exist in English and it is a harder rolled r Similar to *r* in *parachute* when it's placed anywhere else
S	Like *s* in *sit*
T	Like *t* in *tan*
U	Like *u* in *pudding* Silent when it's placed after q and g unless it has a dieresis (ü)
V	Like *v* in *vein*
W	Like *w* in *kiwi*
X	Like *x* in *toxic* In rare occasions it can also sound like *sh* in *ship* or like *h* in *happy*
Y	Like *y* in *May* when it's placed at the end of a word or by itself Like *y* in *yen* when it's placed anywhere else

Z	Like *th* in *think* in Spain
	Like *s* in *super* anywhere else

You should now be able to distinguish the different sounds each letter represents and the special rules on pronunciation depending on their position within a word. Now let's move on to the letter names, so you can be able to spell in Spanish.

Just like we have different pronunciations in English from Australia and English from Scotland, to mention a few, Spanish has minor differences in pronunciation from one region to another which is especially noticeable in the Spanish spoken in the Americas. The sounds given above are for a standard Spanish. We want everyone to understand what you're saying, and you can catch up on the different accents as you progress and meet Spanish speaking people, listen to their music or watch their movies.

Alphabet and letter names

Letter	Name
A	A
B	Be *or* Be alta
C	Ce
D	De

E	E
F	Efe
G	Ge
H	Hache
I	I *or* i latina
J	Jota
K	Ka
L	Ele
M	Eme
N	Ene
Ñ	Eñe
O	O
P	Pe
Q	Cu
R	Ere

S	Ese
T	Te
U	U
V	Ve *or* uve
W	Dobleve *or* Uve doble
X	Equis
Y	Ye *or* Y griega
Z	Zeta

Now you should know the names of the letters so you can spell and you can also pronounce them properly with the examples given in the previous section. You are now super close to being able to read aloud written Spanish, even if you don't know what the words mean... just yet. What's missing? The accents!

Accents

In written Spanish there are implicit and explicit accents to determine which of the syllables within a word is pronounced with more stress. Explicit accents will be the easiest to spot in written form because of their accent marks (á é í ó ú). Let's look at a few examples:

Word	Pronunciation
Canción *(Song)*	can-see-ON
Miércoles *(Wednesday)*	me-ER-coh-less
Ámbar *(Amber)*	AM-bar

Now that was easy, wasn't it? What about words with no explicit accents? How do you know which syllable to stress? Well, you have to follow two simple rules.

If the word doesn't have an accent mark and ends with a consonant, except for *n* and *s*, you will stress the last syllable. Let's look at a few examples.

Word	Pronunciation
Mujer *(Woman)*	moo-HER
Amor *(Love)*	ah-MOR

| Azul | ah-SOOL |

So, what happens if the word doesn't end with a consonant, or if it does with a consonant other than n and s? Well, then you stress the next-to-last syllable. It's that simple!

Word	Pronunciation
Gato *(Cat)*	GAH-toh
Biblio**te**ca *(Library)*	bee-bli-oh-TEH-ca
Puerta	POO-ER-tah

By the end of this lesson and if you've paid attention, you should now be able to read written Spanish pronouncing it correctly. Now it's time to learn some words!

Lesson 2 Greetings and Basic Expressions

To learn a new language you must be familiar with greetings and basic expressions. Take a look at the table below.

Spanish	Pronunciation	English
Hola	OH-lah	Hello
Buenos días	bwe-nos DI-yas	Good morning
Buen día	bwen DI-ya	Good day
Buenas tardes	bwe-nas tar-DES	Good afternoon
Buenas noches	bwe-nas NOH-ches	Good evening / Goodnight

Hasta luego	as-ta LWE-goh	See you later
Chao	cha-OH	Goodbye (informal)
Adiós	ah-dee-OHS	Goodbye
¿Qué tal?	KE tal	What's up?
¿Cómo estás?	KO-mo es-TAS	How are you?
Bien	Byen	Fine
Mal	mal	Bad
Más o menos	MAS oh ME-nos	So-so

These are everyday expressions in Spanish. There is a column with a pronunciation guide so you can practice reading the words aloud.

You might have noticed inverted question and exclamation marks. What's up with them? Well, in Spanish they are used along with regular question and exclamation marks to establish the beginning and the end of a question or exclamation.

Now that you have learned some basic greetings, take a look at this short dialogue.

- ¡Buenos días, Luis!
  Good morning, Luis
- Hola, María. ¿Cómo estás?
  Hello María, how are you?

- Bien, ¿cómo estás tú?
  Fine, how are you?
- Más o menos.
  So-so.

These work wonders if you already know the person you are greeting, but what if you don't know someone? How do you introduce yourself or ask someone's name?

Spanish	Pronunciation	English
¿Cómo te llamas?	KO-mo te LYA-mas	What's your name?
¿Cuál es tu nombre?	ku-AL es tu NOM-bre	What's your name?
Me llamo…	meh-YA-mo	My name is…
Mi nombre es…	me NOM-bre ehs	My name is…
Mucho gusto	MU-cho GUS-toh	Nice to meet you
Es un placer conocerte	es un PLA-ser ko-no-SER-the	It's a pleasure to meet you

"Mi nombre es" literally translates to "My name is", yet in Spanish it's very common to hear and say "me llamo" which literally translates to "I call myself". This might seem odd to you and me, but the verb "llamarse" (to call oneself) is the most used. In the table below you will find it conjugated.

Spanish	English
Me llamo	My name is
Tú te llamas	Your name is
Él se llama	His name is
Ella se llama	Her name is
Esto se llama	Its name is
Nosotros nos llamamos	Our names are
Ustedes se llaman	Your names are (plural)
Ellos se llaman	Their names are

You may have noticed that the pronunciation column is gone in that chart. From now on it will be on and off in some sections so you have to remember and practice the pronunciation rules on lesson 1. Practice makes perfect!

Here are a couple of dialogues for practice.

- Hola, Ramón.
  Hello, Ramón.
- Hola, José, ¿cómo estás?
  Hello, José. How are you?
- Muy bien, gracias.

Very well, thanks.
- Esta es mi amiga. Se llama Sofía.
  This is my friend. Her name is Sofía.
- Mucho gusto, Sofía.
  Nice to meet you, Sofía.

Now let's add a little more vocabulary related to the question "¿cómo estás?".

Spanish	English
Muy bien	Very well
Bien	Well
Regular	So-so
Todo bien	Everything's alright
No muy bien	Not very well
Fatal	Really bad
¿Y tú?	And you?
¿Tú qué tal?	And how are you doing?

You are now familiar with greetings, so let's build up your vocabulary and add more basic expressions.

Spanish	Pronunciation	English
Por favor	por fa-VOR	Please
Gracias	GRA-syas	Thank you
De nada	de na-dha	You're welcome
Por nada	por na-dha	You're welcome
No hay de qué	no ay de keh	You're welcome

You can use *por favor* at the beginning or the end of a phrase when you are asking for something to show respect and good manners.

By now you should know how to pronounce written Spanish, to say your ABC's correctly, with the names of the letters and everything, and now you can also introduce yourself, greet people, bid farewells, ask how they are and tell them how you are doing. You're doing great!

Lesson 3 Numbers, Months, Days and Time

In this lesson you will learn how to say numbers in Spanish as well as months and days of the week.

The numbers

0. Cero
1. Uno
2. Dos
3. Tres
4. Cuatro
5. Cinco
6. Seis
7. Siete
8. Ocho
9. Nueve
10. Diez
11. Once
12. Doce
13. Trece
14. Catorce
15. Quince

Now from number fifteen on, things get super easy. You just have to say "dieci" which is something like "diez y", literally meaning "ten and", followed by the number on the right. Let's take a look.

16. Dieciseis
17. Diecisiete
18. Dieciocho
19. Diecinueve

Isn't that something? Now, from here on, you just have to know the numbers of the tenths, adding "y" and the number on the right. Look.

20. Veinte
21. Veintiuno
22. Veintidos
23. Veintitrés
24. Veinticuatro
25. Veinticinco
26. Veintiseis
27. Veintisiete
28. Veintiocho
29. Veintinueve

As you may have noticed, "Veinte" becomes "veinti", and from then on it's pretty much the same as before. The same happens with the rest of the tenths which are called:

30. Treinta
40. Cuarenta
50. Cincuenta
60. Sesenta
70. Setenta
80. Ochenta
90. Noventa
100. Cien

As you can see, to form the numbers you just take the tenths, add "y" and then add the units.

When you are counting or mentioning a quantity of an object that is masculine, your ones should be "unos", whereas when doing the same for feminine objects you should change your ones to "unas". Now that sounds kind of tricky, but we'll elaborate on it later on.

Let's see some examples.

- Tengo cinco hermanos.
  I have five brothers.

- Hay tres latas de sopa.
  There are three cans of soup

- Tengo veintiocho años.
  I am twenty eight years old.

- Cuesta treinta y cinco dólares.
  It costs thirty five dollars.

- ¿Quieres probar uno?
  Would you like to try one?

Dates

If you want to know what day it is, you can ask "¿Qué día es hoy?" or "¿Qué fecha es hoy?" (*What's the date today?*). But how do you reply if you are the one getting the question? Well, start by saying "Hoy es" which literally translates to "Today is". What about months and the rest? Take a look below.

Months

Spanish	English

Enero	January
Febrero	February
Marzo	March
Abril	April
Mayo	May
Junio	June
Julio	July
Agosto	August
Septiembre	September
Octubre	October
Noviembre	November
Diciembte	December

Days	
Spanish	**English**
Lunes	Monday

Martes	Tuesday
Miércoles	Wednesday
Jueves	Thursday
Viernes	Friday
Sábado	Saturday
Domingo	Sunday

So now you can reply! And this is the little formula on how to do it.

>Hoy es [day of the week], [date] de [month]

So, for example, you could say:

>Hoy es lunes, ocho de junio.
>
>*Today is Monday, 8th of June.*
>
>Hoy es sábado, veintiuno de abril.
>
>*Today is Saturday, 21st of April.*

Did you notice something different from English? In written Spanish you don't have to capitalize the names of the days of the week or the months unless, of course, they are at the beginning of a sentence.

Age and Birthdays

If you want to know someone's age in Spanish, you should ask *¿Qué edad tienes?* (What's your age) or *¿Cuántos años tienes?* (How old are you?).

Now, here's a funny thing. To say ages in Spanish you don't use the same verb we use in English. See, in English we use the "to be" verb. We *are* twenty or thirty years old, while in Spanish you *have* twenty or thirty years.

- Yo tengo veinte años.
  Literal translation: I have twenty seven years.
  Translation: I am twenty seven years old.

- Tú tienes treinta y cuatro años.
  Literal translation: You have thirty four years.
  Translation: You are thirty four years old.

- Él tiene doce años.
  Literal translation: He has twelve years.
  Translation: He is twelve years old.

- Ella tiene tres años.
  Literal translation: She has three years.
  Translation: She is three years old.

- Ustedes tienen cincuenta años.
  Literal translation: You have fifty years.
  Translation: You are fifty years old.

If you want to know when someone's birthday is, you should ask
¿Cuándo es tu cumpleaños? (When's your birthday?).

- ¿Cuándo es tu cumpleaños?
  When's your birthday?
- El trece de marzo, ¿y el tuyo?
  March 13th, when's yours?
- El dieciocho de julio. ¿Cuántos años tienes?
  June 18th. How old are you?
- Tengo diecinueve años. ¿Cuántos años vas a cumplir?
  I am nineteen years old. How old are you going to be?
- Cumpliré 24 años.
  I will be twenty four years old.

Spanish	English
¡Feliz cumpleaños!	Happy birthday!
¿Cuántos años tienes?	How old are you?
¿Qué edad tienes?	What's your age?
¿Cuándo es tu cumpleaños?	When's your birthday?
Tengo ___ años	I am ___ years old
Voy a cumplir ___ años	I will be ___ years old
Cumplo ___ años el veinte de agosto	I will be ___ years old on August 20th

Time

Spanish	English
Año(s)	Year(s)
Mes(es)	Month(s)
Semana(s)	Week(s)
Día(s)	Day(s)
Hora(s)	Hour(s)
Media hora	Half hour
Cuarto de hora	Quarter of an hour
Minuto(s)	Minute(s)
Segundo(s)	Second(s)

If you want to know the time, ask *¿Qué hora es?* (What time is it?). And you can reply as follows:

- Son las cinco de la tarde.
  It's 5PM
- Son las 6 y media.
  It's half past six.
- Son las once y quince.

It's 11:15.
- Son las diez y cuarto.
It's a quarter past ten.
- Son las diez en punto.
It's ten o'clock.
- Es la una y media de la mañana.
It's 1:30AM.

Ordinal Numbers

Ordinal numbers are adjectives that indicate the order of something (first, second, third...) in a series. Unlike the numbers we've seen so far (which are cardinal numbers) these should match the genre and number of the noun or nouns they modify. They are written right before the noun.

Spanish	English
Primero *or* Primer	1st
Segundo	2nd
Tercero	3rd
Cuarto	4th
Quinto	5th
Sexto	6th
Séptimo	7th
Octavo	8th
Noveno	9th
Décimo	10th
Undécimo	11th
Duodécimo	12th
Decimotercero	13th
Decimocuarto	14th
Decimoquinto	15th
Decimosexto	16th
Decimoséptimo	17th
Decimoctavo	18th
Decimonoveno	19th
Vigésimo	20th

Trigésimo	30th
Cuadragésimo	40th
Quincuagésimo	50th
Sexagésimo	60th
Septuagésimo	70th
Octagésimo	80th
Nonagésimo	90th
Centésimo	100th

However, keep in mind that the ordinal numbers *primero* and *tercero* usually drop the "o" when they modify a masculine singular noun.

- El primer día.
  The first day.
- El tercer lugar.
  The third place.

Lesson 4 Nouns: Genders and Plurals

Now that you know what the words sound like, we can start with basic phrases. To do this, of course, you're going to have to know some words and their meaning. But let's go over a couple technical bits, shall we?

Gender

Remember when we told you that Spanish words can either be masculine or feminine, and that we would discuss this further on? Well, the time has come for us to get to it.

This is one of the hardest things to learn but it's also super important to speaking and writing Spanish properly. The gender of the noun will also determine the gender of any adjective you wish to pair it with.

Spanish words can be masculine, feminine or neutral. But how can you distinguish them?

Well, just like before, you just have to follow the rules.

Feminine Nouns

You can tell which nouns are *feminine* because they end with the letters A, D, Z or the syllable "ción".

Take a look:

Spanish	English
Agua	Water
Amiga	Female Friend
Canción	Song
Chica	Girl
Deidad	Deity
Dramatización	Dramatization
Felicidad	Happiness
Flor	Flower
Fruta	Fruit

Guitarra	Guitar
Piscina	Pool
Puerta	Door
Revista	Magazine
Rosa	Rose
Salud	Health
Universidad	University
Ventana	Window

So what does this mean? This means that whenever you want to say something regarding a feminine noun, you should also use a feminine definite article (la) and feminine adjectives.

Here are a few examples:

- La rosa es blanca.
  The rose is white.
- La chica tiene doce años.
  The girl is 12 years old.
- La revista es muy buena.
  The magazine is very good.
- La ventana es grande.
  The window is big.
- La piscina está fría.
  The pool is cold.
- La guitarra es nueva.
  The guitar is new.

Masculine Nouns

You can tell which nouns are *masculine* because they end with the letters E, L, N, O, R or the syllables "es", "is", "os" and "us".

Here are a few:

Spanish	English
Amigo	Male Friend
Árbol	Tree
Autobús	Bus
Bebé	Baby
Documento	Document
Hombre	Man
Jamón	Ham
Jugo	Juice
Lapicero	Pen
Limón	Lemon
Miedo	Fear
País	Country
Papel	Paper

Pastel	Cake
Perro	Dog
Ratón	Mouse
Tazón	Bowl
Vestido	Dress

And again, what does this mean? This means that whenever you want to say something regarding a masculine noun, you should also use a masculine definite article (el) and masculine adjectives.

Here are a few examples:

- El perro se llama Pepe.
  The dog's name is Pepe.
- El pastel está caliente.
  The cake is hot.
- El vestido es negro.
  The dress is black.
- El tazón está lleno.
  The bowl is full.
- El país es grande.
  The country is big.
- El bebé es lindo.
  The baby is cute.

Neutral Nouns

Neutral nouns are those who can be either masculine or feminine, depending on the actual gender of the person you're talking about. These do not follow any specific rules, so this time you are on your own and must memorize them. Here are a few:

Spanish	English

Artista	Artist
Deportista	Athlete
Futbolista	Football player
Gerente	Manager
Guitarrista	Guitarist
Pianista	Pianist
Representante	Representative

If you are reading written Spanish, you can cheat a little. Every noun in Spanish is preceded by a specific article, so if you read "la" (singular) or "las" (plural) you can be sure that the noun is feminine. However, if you instead read "el" (singular) or "los" (plural) you can be 100% positive that the noun is masculine. Pretty neat, huh?

You will also notice that some nouns can be used as masculine or feminine. For example, *un gato* is a male cat, while *una gata* is a female cat. The same happens to most animal names in Spanish, except for a few exceptions.

You must always remember NOT to follow your gut when trying to guess the gender of a noun in Spanish. Your brain will play tricks on you. See, if I tell you that a tie is called *corbata*, your gut will directly think tie → man → masculine and say something like "*el *corbata*", which is completely wrong. So remember to stop, remember the rules and then assign the noun's gender correctly.

Plural

Just like in English, nouns in Spanish change when you are referring to singular or plural subjects. For the most part, these are super easy. Guess what you have to learn in order to get these correctly? Yup, rules, rules and more rules!

Rule number one: Add "s" at the end of any word ending with a vowel.

Singular	Plural	Meaning
Ave	Aves	Bird(s)
Calle	Calles	Street(s)
Casa	Casas	House(s)
Gato	Gatos	Cat(s)
Manzana	Manzanas	Apple(s)
Niño	Niños	Boy(s)
Perro	Perros	Dog(s)
Piña	Piñas	Pineapple(s)
Sala	Salas	Room(s)

Rule number two: Add "es" at the end of any word ending with a consonant other than z.

Singular	Plural	Meaning
Ciudad	Ciudades	City/Cities
Flor	Flores	Flower(s)
Habitación	Habitaciones	Room(s)
Hotel	Hoteles	Hotel(s)
Mes	Meses	Month(s)
Papel	Papeles	Paper(s)
Reloj	Relojes	Clock(s)
Señor	Señores	Sir(s)
Tazón	Tazones	Bowl(s)

Rule number three: If a word ends in z, change "z" for a "c" and then add "es" at the end.

Singular	Plural	Meaning
Barniz	Barnices	Varnish(es)
Codorniz	Codornices	Quail(s)
Lápiz	Lápices	Pencil(s)
Luz	Luces	Light(s)
Matiz	Matices	Hue(s)
Pez	Peces	Fish(es)
Voz	Voces	Voice(s)

That's not so hard to remember, is it? Now, as usual, there are a few exceptions to these rules. For example, days of the week (remember those, on the previous lesson?) ending in "s" remain as they are when pluralized, and you only get to add "s" to pluralize *sábados* (Saturdays) and *domingos* (Sundays).

Free Course – Speak in a Week!

Congratulations on making it this far. It's a sad fact that most people never make it past the first few pages of a book, but you are the exception!

Since you're committed to learning Spanish, I would like to give you a free 7 day course called *Speak in a Week*. Visit http://www.deepthoughtpress.com/speak-in-a-week to enroll now for free. You'll be joining the 100,000+ language hackers that have already taken this course.

You'll start speaking Spanish in just seven days - no matter what your skill level. Visit:

http://www.deepthoughtpress.com/speak-in-a-week

Thanks! Now on to articles and pronouns...

Lesson 5 Articles and Pronouns

Bear with us. We know the last lesson was a bit tough and the title for this one is not particularly attractive, but learning Spanish is like solving a big puzzle. Little by little things will become clearer and easier to understand and memorize.

Articles

Remember when we talked about nouns and their genders? Well, let's recap. When writing or speaking Spanish the genres of your nouns must match the genders of your adjectives and articles. They should also be adjusted in singular and plural.

Just like in English, there are definite and indefinite articles in Spanish.

Nouns are usually preceded by an article, which can be definite or indefinite. In case you need to refresh this, in English the definite article is "the", which is amazing because it works for anything, singular and plural. However, in Spanish there are multiple definite articles.

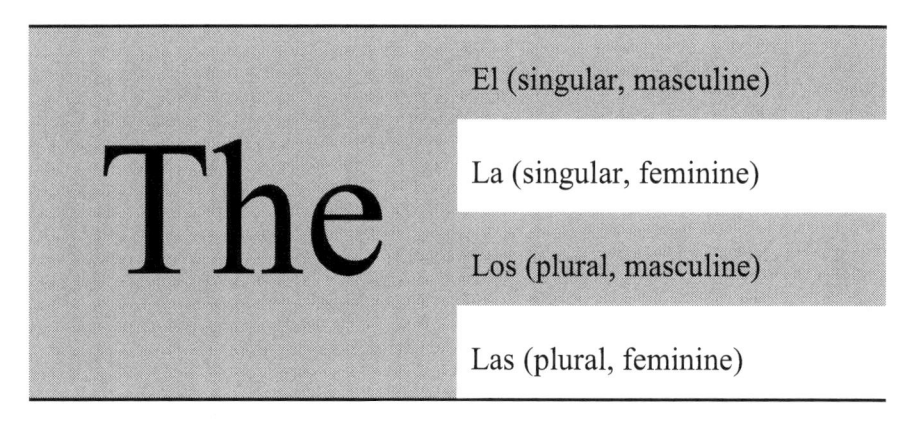

The	El (singular, masculine)
	La (singular, feminine)
	Los (plural, masculine)
	Las (plural, feminine)

Indefinite articles in English are "a", "an" and "some". In Spanish, you simply use number one with the slight variation for gender and plurality we mentioned earlier. Take a look:

A/An	Un (singular, masculine)
	Una (singular, feminine)
Some	Unos (plural, masculine)
	Unas (plural, feminine)

So it's quite simple. First identify the gender of the noun, then identify if it's singular or plural, and finally determine if you want to add a definite or indefinite article, and you're set!

With what you have learned in the lessons combined so far, you can now form very short nominal phrases. Isn't that awesome?

- Diez flores.
  Ten flowers.
- Una casa.
  A house.
- Cien dólares.
  A hundred dollars.
- Ocho días.
  Eight days.
- Cuatro meses.
  Four months.
- Dos manzanas y un durazno.
  Two apples and a peach.
- El niño y dos amigos.
  The boy and two friends.
- Unos muchachos y dos maestros.
  Some boys and two teachers.

Pronouns

Pronouns in Spanish, just like in English, are used to substitute nouns in phrases or paragraphs when you don't want to repeat them over and over again.

Sometimes the pronouns can be implied. In Spanish the verbs can sometimes contain both the person and number of the subject. Does that sound complicated? It's really not, but we'll get to it soon.

Subject Pronouns

Take a look at the subject pronouns in this chart:

Spanish	English
Yo	I
Tú/Usted	You
El	He
Ella	She
Este/Esta	It
Nosotros (m) / Nosotras (f)	We
Ustedes/Vosotros	You
Ellos (m) / Ellas (f)	They

Okay, so the first five pronouns are singular pronouns for the first, second and third person, while the remaining pronouns are plural for the first, second and third person.

These are quite simple and work pretty much the same as they do in English with minor differences. Did you notice there are two words separated by a slash on the second person in singular?

Well, that's because in Spanish, when talking to someone you can either use the informal pronoun or the formal one.

The informal pronoun (*tú, ustedes*) is used when you are talking to someone who is close to you, a relative or a friend, or people around the same age as you are. In some countries or regions you will find that people use *vos* instead of *tú*. That is completely normal, yet we are teaching you *tú* because it's most widely said and understood by everyone.

However, if you are talking to a stranger, perhaps someone older than you are, or maybe your boss or an authority, you should use the formal version to show respect (*usted*).

You will also see there are two words for the second and third person in plural. But we know you are super smart and you could tell that they are different for masculine or feminine subjects!

However, there's something we haven't told you about Spanish and plural. When you are referring to a singular feminine subject, you can of course use a feminine plural. Take a look.

La mujer	→	Las mujeres
Ella	→	Ellas

And if you are referring to a singular masculine subject, the same applies.

El hombre	→	Los hombres
El	→	Ellos

Now, what happens if you talk about a mixed group of people? And you need a neutral plural pronoun? You use the same you would as if they were all masculine.

    El hombre y la mujer =　　　El y ella　　=　　　Ellos

You should now be familiar with the subject pronouns. You'll see more about them when we get to build more phrases. You're doing great so far!

Possesive Pronouns

Now let's take a look at the possessive pronouns:

Spanish	English
Mi(s)	My
Tu(s)	Your
Su(s)	
Su(s)	His
Su(s)	Her
Su(s)	Its
Nuestro(s)	Our
Su(s)	Your
Su(s)	Their

If you didn't remember these, these are the pronouns used to show ownership. Just like everything else in Spanish they depend on the gender and number of the subjects in the same sentence.

Not only can you now form basic sentences, but you can even try to write or say small paragraphs. Look at these examples.

- Ella es mi mamá.
  She is my mom.
- Él es Juan. Juan es mi amigo.
  He is Juan. Juan is my friend.
- Esta pelota es de María. Es su pelota.
  This is María's ball. It is her ball.

Demonstratives

As you may have guessed, demonstratives are used to refer to nouns or subjects depending to how far or close they are from us. As with everything else you've learned so far, they work pretty much as they do in English, but they have little adjustments according to the genre of the subject they are referring to.

Feminine	Masculine	Meaning
Esta	Este	This
Esa	Ese	That
Estas	Estos	These

Esas	Esos	Those
Aquellos	Aquellas	

The demonstratives in gray are plural. You may have noticed that *those* can be said in two different ways. These are pretty much the same

Let's take a look at a few examples.

- Este perro.
  This dog.
- Esta casa.
  This house.
- Ese muchacho.
  That boy.
- Aquellas flores.
  Those flowers.
- Estas vacas.
  These cows.
- Aquellos días.
  Those days.

Now you should even be able to build small paragraphs such as this one.

- Hola. Este es mi amigo. Su nombre es José.
  Hello. This is my friend. His name is José.
- Estas son mis hermanas. Tienen trece años.
  These are my sisters. They are thirteen years old.

Lesson 6 Adjectives

Adjectives are used to describe or modify subjects. As you've seen with everything else, they may change depending on if the nouns they modify are feminine or masculine and if they are singular or plural. This is the same as you have seen for pronouns and articles.

The trick to using adjectives properly is to find the noun and determine its genre and its number.

Most of the times you will find descriptive adjectives. This means they are used to describe a noun or to highlight their characteristics so you can tell them apart from a group of similar things or objects.

Most of the times you'll find the adjectives right after the nouns, which will probably seem a bit odd since they always come before the nouns in English. The thing is in Spanish it doesn't really make much of a difference, and there are cases when you might find the adjective before the noun.

This might seem confusing, but you'll get the hang of it as you practice. Take a look at these examples:

- El gato naranja
  The orange cat
- Las niñas felices
  The happy girls
- El hombre joven
  The young man
- Las mujeres altas
  The tall women
- Las casas grandes
  The big houses
- Los automóviles rápidos
  The fast cars
- Los perros bravos
  The mad dogs
- Las serpientes rojas
  The red snakes
- Las bolsas pequeñas
  The small bags
- Los libros nuevos
  The new books

Neuter adjectives

These should be the easiest to use and remember. Neuter adjectives don't change according to the genre of the subject, and then you only have to change them a bit depending on the number of the subject. That's quite easy, remember? You just have to add "es" or "s" at the end and it's done.

Most neuter adjectives end with a consonant or the letter "e".

- El niño inteligente
  The smart boy
- La niña inteligente
  The smart girl
- El perro común
  The common dog
- La vaca común
  The common cow
- Los niños inteligentes
  The smart boys
- Las niñas inteligentes
  The smart girls
- Los perros comunes
  The common dogs
- Las vacas comunes
  The common cows

Regular adjectives

These are a bit harder, but you are almost an expert by now. They follow the same rules you have seen before regarding the genre and number of the noun, so it's nothing too complicated. And they will always end in "a", "o", "as" or "os". Take a look.

- El perro flaco
  The thin dog (male)
- La perra flaca
  The thin dog (female)
- La chica nueva
  The new girl
- El chico nuevo
  The new boy
- Los perros flacos
  The thin dogs (male)
- Las perras flacas

- *The thin dogs (female)*
- Las chicas nuevas
The new girls

- Los chicos nuevos
The new boys

Now, to build your vocabulary, here are some adjectives. We have highlighted *neutral adjectives* so you can spot them easily.

Descriptive Adjectives

Singular	Plural	Meaning
Absurdo	Absurdos	Absurd
Aburrido	Aburridos	Boring
Actual	Actuales	Current
Agresivo	Agresivos	Aggressive
Alegre	Alegres	Glad
Alto	Altos	Tall
Amable	Amables	Nice
Amargo	Amargos	Bitter
Angular	Angulares	Angled
Ansioso	Ansiosos	Anxious
Apacible	Apacibles	Pleasant
Asqueroso	Asquerosos	Disgusting
Asustado	Asustados	Scared
Baboso	Babosos	Slimy
Barato	Baratos	Cheap
Básico	Básicos	Basic
Bello	Bellos	Beautiful
Bonito	Bonitos	Pretty
Borracho	Borrachos	Drunk
Brillante	Brillantes	Shiny
Brillante	Brillantes	Bright
Bueno	Buenos	Good
Caliente	Calientes	Hot
Caliente	Calientes	Hot
Cansado	Cansados	Tired
Capaz	Capaces	Able, capable
Capaz	Capaces	Able
Cariñoso	Cariñosos	Loving
Caro	Caros	Expensive
Casado	Casados	Married
Celoso	Celosos	Jealous
Chistoso	Chistosos	Funny
Ciego	Ciegos	Blind
Cilíndrico	Cilíndricos	Cylindrical
Claro	Claros	Clear
Comestible	Comestibles	Edible
Cómico	Cómicos	Funny
Común	Comunes	Common
Confortable	Confortables	Comfortable
Confortable	Confortables	Comfortable

Conservador	Conservadores	Conservative
Contento	Contentos	Glad
Correcto	Correctos	Correct
Corriente	Corrientes	Common
Cortante	Cortantes	Sharp
Cortés	Corteses	Courteous
Corto	Cortos	Short
Creativo	Creativos	Creative
Crudo	Crudos	Raw
Cruel	Crueles	Cruel
Cuadrado	Cuadrados	Square
Cuidadoso	Cuidadosos	Careful
Culpable	Culpables	Guilty
Curioso	Curiosos	Curious
Débil	Débiles	Weak
Delgado	Delgados	Thin
Delicioso	Deliciosos	Delicious
Deprimido	Deprimidos	Depressed
Descortés	Descorteses	Discorteous
Descortés	Descorteses	Discourteous
Desesperado	Desesperados	Desperate
Deshonesto	Deshonestos	Dishonest
Desnudo	Desnudos	Naked
Despacio	Despacios	Slow
Distinto	Distintos	Distinct
Divertido	Divertidos	Fun
Divorciado	Divorciados	Divorced
Doloroso	Dolorosos	Painful
Doméstico	Domésticos	Domestic
Duro	Duros	Hard
Enamorado	Enamorados	Enamoured
Enfermo	Enfermos	Sick
Enojado	Enojados	Angry
Especial	Especiales	Special
Evitable	Evitables	Avoidable
Excelente	Excelentes	Excellent
Exótico	Exóticos	Exotic
Extraño	Extraños	Strange
Fantástico	Fantásticos	Fantastic
Favorito	Favoritos	Favorite
Feliz	Felices	Happy
Feo	Feos	Ugly
Feroz	Feroces	Ferocious
Flaco	Flacos	Thin
Flexible	Flexibles	Flexible
Flojo	Flojos	Lazy

Formal	Formales	Formal
Frágil	Frágiles	Fragile
Fresco	Frescos	Cool
Frío	Fríos	Cold
Frito	Fritos	Fried
Frustrado	Frustrados	Frustrated
Fuerte	Fuertes	Strong
General	Generales	General
Gordo	Gordos	Fat
Grande	Grandes	Big
Grave	Graves	Severe, Critical
Grueso	Gruesos	Thick
Guapo	Guapos	Handsome
Hermoso	Hermosos	Beautiful
Hervido	Hervidos	Boiled
Hinchado	Hinchados	Swollen
Honesto	Honestos	Honest
Horrible	Horribles	Horrible
Húmedo	Húmedos	Humid
Ignorante	Ignorantes	Ignorant
Igual	Iguales	Equal
Ilegal	Ilegales	Illegal
Impaciente	Impacientes	Impatient
Imposible	Imposibles	Impossible
Impresionable	Impresionables	Impressionable
Improbable	Improbables	Improbable
Incapaz	Incapaces	Incapable
Incorrecto	Incorrectos	Wrong
Increíble	Increíbles	Incredible
Increíble	Increíbles	Incredible
Infeliz	Infelices	Unhappy
Inferior	Inferiores	Inferior
Inferior	Inferiores	Inferior
Inocente	Inocentes	Innocent
Inocente	Inocentes	Innocent
Inolvidable	Inolvidables	Unforgettable
Instantáneo	Instantáneos	Instant
Inteligente	Inteligentes	Smart, Intelligent
Interesante	Interesantes	Interesting
Intolerable	Intolerables	Intolerable
Intolerante	Intolerantes	Intolerant
Inútil	Inútiles	Useless
Invisible	Invisibles	Invisible
Irresponsable	Irresponsables	Irresponsible
Joven	Jóvenes	Young
Largo	Largos	Long

Legal	Legales	Legal
Lento	Lentos	Slow
Liberal	Liberales	Liberal
Libre	Libres	Free
Ligero	Ligeros	Light
Limpio	Limpios	Clean
Liso	Lisos	Smooth
Listo	Listos	Ready, Smart
Lleno	Llenos	Full
Loco	Locos	Crazy
Maduro	Maduros	Ripe, Mature
Magnífico	Magníficos	Magnificent
Malo	Malos	Bad
Mediano	Medianos	Medium
Mejor	Mejores	Better
Miserable	Miserables	Miserable
Miserable	Miserables	Miserable
Mojado	Mojados	Damp
Móvil	Móviles	Mobile
Natural	Naturales	Natural
Normal	Normales	Normal
Nuevo	Nuevos	New
Obvio	Obvios	Obvious
Organizado	Organizados	Organized
Orgulloso	Orgullosos	Proud
Oscuro	Oscuros	Dark
Paciente	Pacientes	Patient
Pálido	Pálidos	Pale
Peligroso	Peligrosos	Dangerous
Pequeño	Pequeños	Small
Perdido	Perdidos	Lost
Perezoso	Perezosos	Lazy
Pesado	Pesados	Heavy
Picante	Picantes	Spicy
Plano	Planos	Flat
Pobre	Pobres	Poor
Poco	Pocos	Few
Posible	Posibles	Possible
Positivo	Positivos	Positive
Precioso	Preciosos	Precious
Preocupado	Preocupados	Worried
Probable	Probables	Probable
Probable	Probables	Probable
Profundo	Profundos	Deep
Promedio	Promedios	Average
Puntual	Puntuales	Punctual

Puro	Puros	Pure
Quemado	Quemados	Burnt
Querido	Queridos	Dear
Quieto	Quietos	Still
Rápido	Rápidos	Fast
Redondo	Redondos	Round
Responsable	Responsables	Responsible
Ridículo	Ridículos	Ridiculous
Roto	Rotos	Broken
Ruidoso	Ruidosos	Noisy
Sabio	Sabios	Wise
Sabroso	Sabrosos	Tasty
Salvaje	Salvajes	Wild
Seco	Secos	Dry
Sentimental	Sentimentales	Sentimental
Severo	Severos	Severe
Simpático	Simpáticos	Nice
Sincero	Sinceros	Honest
Sordo	Sordos	Deaf
Sorprendente	Sorprendentes	Surprising
Sospechoso	Sospechosos	Suspicious
Sucio	Sucios	Dirty
Superior	Superiores	Superior
Terrible	Terribles	Terrible
Terrible	Terribles	Terrible
Tibio	Tibios	Warm
Tolerable	Tolerables	Tolerable
Tolerante	Tolerante	Tolerant
Tolerante	Tolerantes	Tolerant
Tonto	Tontos	Dumb
Tranquilo	Tranquilos	Peaceful
Travieso	Traviesos	Naughty
Triste	Tristes	Sad
Triste	Tristes	Sad
Único	Únicos	Unique
Usado	Usados	Used
Útil	Útiles	Useful
Útil	Útiles	Useful
Vacío	Vacíos	Empty
Venenoso	Venenosos	Poisonous
Vergonzoso	Vergonzosos	Embarrassing
Viejo	Viejos	Old
Vulgar	Vulgares	Vulgar

Colors

Here is a short list of colors. Again, you will see neutral adjectives highlighted below.

Singular	Plural	Meaning
Amarillo	Amarillos	Yellow
Azul	Azules	Blue
Blanco	Blancos	White
Café	Cafés	Brown
Claro	Claros	Light
Dorado	Dorados	Golden
Gris	Grises	Gray
Marrón	Marrones	Brown
Morado	Morados	Purple
Naranja	Naranjas	Orange
Negro	Negros	Black
Oscuro	Oscuros	Dark
Plateado	Plateados	Silver
Rojo	Rojos	Red
Rosa	Rosas	Pink
Verde	Verdes	Green
Violeta	Violetas	Violet

Nationalities

These adjectives are probably the trickiest so far. No rules to follow either, so you guessed: you have to memorize them. Here is a short list.

Singular	Plural	Meaning
Alemán	Alemanes	German
Argentino	Argentinos	Argentinean
Boliviano	Bolivianos	Bolivian
Brasilero	Brasileros	Brazilian
Británico	Británicos	British
Canadiense	Canadienses	Canadian
Chileno	Chilenos	Chilean
Chino	Chinos	Chinese
Colombiano	Colombianos	Colombian
Costarricense	Costarricenses	Costa Rican
Cubano	Cubanos	Cuban
Ecuatoriano	Ecuatorianos	Ecuadorian
Egipcio	Egipcios	Egyptian
Escocés	Escoceses	Scottish
Español	Españoles	Spanish
Estadounidense	Estadounidenses	American
Francés	Franceses	French
Griego	Griegos	Greek
Guatemalteco	Guatemaltecos	Guatemalan
Holandés	Holandeses	Dutch
Hondureño	Hondureños	Honduran
Inglés	Ingleses	English
Irlandés	Irlandeses	Irish
Italiano	Italianos	Italian
Japonés	Japoneses	Japanese
Mexicano	Mexicanos	Mexicans
Nicaragüense	Nicaragüenses	Nicaraguan
Paraguayo	Paraguayos	Paraguayan
Peruano	Peruanos	Peruvian
Polaco	Polacos	Polish
Portugués	Portugueses	Portuguese
Puertorriqueño	Puertorriqueños	Puerto Rican
Ruso	Rusos	Russian
Salvadoreño	Salvadoreños	Salvadorian
Sueco	Suecos	Swedish
Suizo	Suizos	Swiss
Uruguayo	Uruguayos	Uruguayan
Venezolano	Venezolanos	Venezuelan

By the end of this lesson you should be able to distinguish which adjectives are neuter (having only two forms, according to the number of the noun they modify) and which are regular (having four forms, according to genre and number.

Now you should be able to form more elaborate phrases! Look at the examples below.

- El perro grande.
  The big dog.
- Té inglés.
  English tea.
- Mi amigo sueco.
  My Swedish friend.
- El primer auto, el azul.
  The first car, the blue one.
- Las primeras veces.
  The first times.
- El tercer cajón.
  The third drawer.
- La cuarta casa.
  The fourth house.
- Mis pantalones negros.
  My black pants.
- Tus manzanas verdes.
  Your green apples.

Lesson 7 Prepositions and Seasons

Prepositions

Prepositions in Spanish are very easy to understand since they are used just as they are in English. They are used to indicate a relationship between two other words and usually indicate a direction, place or time. Prepositions can be either simple (one word) or compound (multiple words).

Using prepositions is very important to form phrases. Let's go through the most common prepositions. Take a look.

Spanish	English
A	At
	By means of
	To
Antes de	Before
Bajo	Under
Debajo de	
Con	With
Contra	Against
De	From
	Of
Delante de	In front of
Dentro de	Inside of
Desde	From
	Since
Después de	After
Detrás de	Behind
Durante	During
En	At
	In
	On
Encima de	Above
	On top of
Enfrente de	In front of
Entre	Between
Fuera de	Outside of
Hacia	Towards
Hasta	Until
Para	For
	In order to
Por	By
	For
Según	According to
Sin	Without
Sobre	About
	Over

Okay, so most of the times you will notice that prepositions in Spanish are used pretty much as we use them in English. See how some of them have several translations? How do you tell what they mean? Well, you have to figure it out from the context. Don't get scared! It sounds far more complicated than it really is. You just need to practice.

Let's look at some examples, shall we?

- A la playa.
  To the beach.
- A las cinco y media.
  At five and a half.
- A pie.
  On foot.
- Antes del almuerzo.
  Before lunch.
- Bajo la cama.
  Under the bed.
- Cerca de mi casa.
  Near my house.
- Azul con puntos rojos.
  Blue with red dots.
- Contra el crimen.
  Against crime.
- Barco de papel.
  Paper boat. (Lit. translation: Boat of paper)
- Avión de Argentina.
  Plane from Argentina.
- El color de sus ojos.
  The color of his/her/its eyes.
- Delante de José.
  In front of José.
- Dentro de la casa.
  Inside the house.
- Desde las dos y media.
  Since two and a half.
- Desde tu escuela.
  From your school.
- Después de las seis de la tarde.
  After 6PM.
- Encima de nuestra mesa.
  On our table.
- Enfrente del espejo.
  In front of the mirror.
- Entre el verde y el naranja.
  Between the green and the orange one.
- Fuera de la caja.
  Out of the box.
- Hacia los árboles.
  Towards the trees.
- Hasta los hombros.
  To the shoulders.
- Para Mariana.
  For Mariana.
- Gracias por la carta.
  Thank you for the letter.
- El libro por Tolkien.
  The book by Tolkien.
- Según los estudios.
  According to the studies.
- Sin azúcar.
  Without sugar.
- Sobre la silla.
  On the chair.
- Un artículo sobre los caballos.
  An article about horses.

Seasons

In Spanish you will mostly find seasons preceded by articles (remember those? *"el", "la", "los", "las"*). Here are four more words for your vocabulary!

Spanish	English
Primavera	Spring
Verano	Summer
Otoño	Autumn
Invierno	Winter

Lesson 8 Verbs in the Present Tense

Things just got serious, my friend. Spanish verbs are one of the most complicated topics about the language. However, they are just what you need in order to form more complex phrases. First of all, keep in mind that you will be able to spot Spanish verbs because every verb (in infinitive form, whatsoever) ends with the syllables "ar", "er" or "ir."

We can classify Spanish verbs according to the syllable they end with, since they follow similar conjugation patterns and rules depending on that.

To keep things simple, we will only tackle some basic verbs in present tense. You definitely need these foundations to learn the rest of them.

"Ar" verbs

You're going to need to learn to conjugate the verbs. There's not really much to do with verbs in infinitive form when it comes to forming phrases. Take a look at the example below.

Hablar (to speak)

Spanish	English
Yo hablo…	I speak…
Tú hablas…	You speak…
Él habla…	He speaks…
Ella habla…	She speaks…
Esto habla…	It speaks…
Nosotros hablamos…	We speak…
Ustedes hablan…	You speak…
Ellos hablan…	They speak…

Did you notice the slight differences? Pretty easy, right? Well, now here's something else: verbs in Spanish can contain the subject, which means you will find sentences which totally omit personal pronouns, yet you can still tell who the subject is. Kind of. Take a look at the same verb.

Spanish	English
Hablo…	I speak…
Hablas…	You speak…
Habla…	He speaks…
Habla…	She speaks…
Habla…	It speaks…
Hablamos…	We speak…
Hablan…	You speak…
Hablan…	They speak…

Do you see the pattern? You can use that pattern with any verb finishing with the syllable "ar". Or well, almost any verb. As usual, there are a few exceptions. By now we won't talk about those irregular verbs. Take a look at the examples below.

Verb	Example
Caminar *(to walk)*	Yo camino a la escuela. Camino a la escuela. *I walk to school.*
Estudiar *(to study)*	Tú estudias francés. Estudias francés. *Lit. Translation: You study French – You are taking French*
Borrar *(to erase)*	Él/Ella borra la pizarra. Borra la pizarra. *He/She erases the blackboard.*
Bailar *(to dance)*	Nosotros bailamos salsa. Bailamos salsa. *We dance salsa.*
Cocinar *(to cook)*	Ustedes cocinan sopa. Cocinan sopa. *You (pl) cook soup.*
Saludar *(to greet)*	Ellos saludan a los invitados. Saludan a los invitados. *They greet the guests.*

See? It's the exact same modifications. Now here's a list of basic "ar" verbs for you to memorize.

Spanish	English
Aceptar	To accept
Acompañar	To accompany
Aconsejar	To advise
Arreglar	To arrange
	To fix
Ayudar	To help
Bailar	To dance
Bajar	To go down
Borrar	To erase
	To delete
Caminar	To walk
Cantar	To sing
Celebrar	To celebrate
Cenar	To eat dinner
	To have dinner
Cocinar	To cook
Comprar	To buy
Contestar	To answer
Cortar	To cut
Dejar	To leave
Desear	To wish
	To want
Empujar	To push
Entrar	To enter
	To come in
Escuchar	To listen to
Estudiar	To study
Firmar	To sign
Ganar	To win
	To earn
Gastar	To spend
Gritar	To shout
Hablar	To speak
Invitar	To invite
Llamar	To call
Llevar	To bring
	To wear
Llorar	To cry

Mandar	To send
	To order/command
Mirar	To look
Nadar	To swim
Necesitar	To need
Parar	To stop
Pasar	To pass
Patinar	To skate
Pintar	To paint
Preguntar	To ask
Preparar	To prepare
Presentar	To present
Quitar	To take off
	To remove
Regresar	To return
Saludar	To greet
Terminar	To end
	To finish
Tirar	To throw
Tocar	To play
Tomar	To take
	To drink
Trabajar	To work
Usar	To use
	To wear

"Er" verbs

Conjugating verbs that end with the syllable "er" is fairly simple. Once you see and memorize the pattern, you'll be able to conjugate them. Take a look.

Comer (to eat)

Spanish	English
Yo com**o**…	I eat…
Tú com**es**…	You eat…
Él com**e**…	He eats…
Ella com**e**…	She eats…
Esto com**e**…	This eats…
Nosotros com**emos**…	We eat…
Ustedes com**en**…	You eat…
Ellos com**en**…	They eat…

See the pattern on this one? Alright, then let's see how it looks like when the subject is omitted.

Spanish	English
Com**o**…	I eat…
Com**es**…	You eat…
Com**e**…	He eats…
Com**e**…	She eats…
Com**e**…	This eats…
Com**emos**…	We eat…
Com**en**…	You eat…
Com**en**…	They eat…

Just like before, you can use the same pattern when you encounter almost every other verbs finishing with the syllable "er". Let's see some examples.

Verb	Example
Comer *(to eat)*	Yo como naranjas. Como naranjas. *I eat oranges.*
Beber *(to drink)*	Tú bebes agua. Bebes agua. *You drink water.*
Correr *(to run)*	El/Ella corre los martes. Corre los martes. *He/She runs on Tuesdays.*
Leer *(to read)*	Nosotros leemos novelas de misterio. Leemos novelas de misterio. *We read mystery novels.*
Vender *(to sell)*	Ustedes venden llaveros. Venden llaveros. *You (pl) sell keychains.*
Aprender *(to learn)*	Ellos aprenden español. Aprenden español. *They learn Spanish.*

Now here's a list of basic "er" verbs for you to memorize.

Spanish	English
Aprender	To learn
Barrer	To sweep
Beber	To drink
Comer	To eat
Comprender	To comprehend/understand
Correr	To run
Deber	To go down
	To erase
Leer	To delete
Meter	To walk
	To light/turn on
Prender	To catch
Romper	To break
Temer	To fear
Toser	To cough

Vender	To sell

"Ir" verbs

There are not many verbs ending with the syllable "ir". These you will find pretty simple since the conjugation is very similar to that of "er" verbs. Let's see some examples.

Escribir (to write)

Spanish	English
Yo escrib**o**…	I write…
Tú escrib**es**…	You write…
Él escrib**e**…	He writes…
Ella escrib**e**…	She writes…
Esto escrib**e**…	This writes…
Nosotros escrib**imos**…	We write…
Ustedes escrib**en**…	You write…
Ellos escrib**en**…	They write…

See the pattern on this one? The only difference is on the first person in plural. All good? Then let's take a look at them with omitted subjects.

Spanish	English
Escrib**o**…	I write…
Escrib**es**…	You write…
Escrib**e**…	He writes…
Escrib**e**…	She writes…
Escrib**e**…	This writes…
Escrib**imos**…	We write…
Escrib**en**…	You write…
Escrib**en**…	They write…

Let's see some examples and other verbs.

Verb	Example
Abrir *(to open)*	Yo abro la puerta. Abro la puerta. *I open the door.*
Descubrir *(to discover)*	Tú descubres pistas. Descubres pistas. *You discover clues.*
Escribir *(to write)*	El/Ella escribe cartas. Escribe cartas. *He/She writes letters.*
Discutir *(to discuss)*	Nosotros discutimos temas interesantes. Discutimos temas interesantes. *We discuss interesting topics.*
Subir *(to go up/get on)*	Ustedes suben al autobús. Suben al autobús. *You (pl) get on the bus.*
Vivir *(to live)*	Ellos viven en esa casa. Viven en esa casa. *They live in that house.*

And here are some "ir" verbs.

Spanish	English
Abrir	To open
Coincidir	To coincide
Conseguir	To find/accomplish
Decidir	To decide
Decir	To say
Escribir	To write
Exigir	To demand
Existir	To exist
Pedir	To ask for/order/request
Recibir	To receive
Seguir	To follow/continue
Sentir	To feel
Subir	To go up
Sufrir	To suffer
Vivir	To live

By the end of this lessons you should be able to apply everything you've learned so far to form longer and more complicated phrases or even brief paragraphs. Bravo! Take a look at these examples:

- Juan viene de visita. Es la primera vez que viene a esta casa. Mi mamá quiere hablar con él.
  Juan comes to visit. It is the first time he comes to this house.
- Ana tiene un perro negro y grande.
- Nos gusta el helado de mora. Ellos quieren helado de vainilla.
  We like blackberry ice cream. They want vanilla ice cream.

Summary

You have now reached the end of this book! We really hope you had fun with these lessons and are now able to write and say phrases in Spanish! It has been a long way from the ABC's and pronunciation to conjugating verbs. Well done! Remember the rules we taught you in each lesson and keep on practicing. Also, remember that practice makes perfect and you will speak Spanish fluently in no time!

We want to congratulate you on embarking on your journey to learning Spanish. Despite the common belief, learning Spanish does not have to be difficult and complicated. It can be fun and fast if you memorize and follow our little rules and tricks!

You have learned basic Spanish in just a week, and that's amazing. We want to encourage you to keep learning and improving your pronunciation.

We wish you the best. *¡Adiós!*

Additional Resources for Further Study

Speak in a Week
http://www.deepthoughtpress.com/speak-in-a-week

Join 100,000+ language hackers in this free course where you'll start speaking your target language in just seven days - no matter what your skill level.

Why Spanish is Easy
http://www.deepthoughtpress.com/spanish-is-easy

In the book you'll learn:

- Why learning Spanish can be easier than learning French, German, Latin or even English
- Simple ways to immerse yourself in Spanish without the need to travel
- How to use goals and missions to build momentum in your language learning
- How to roll your R and other pronunciation difficulties

- How to handle Spanish grammar, so you can start speaking without wondering "how do I say..?" (For grammar geeks, I provide tips on noun genders, verb conjugation, subjunctive and more)
- Very easy ways to remember when to use ser or estar, and por or para
- How to understand Spanish spoken by native speakers and how to find native speakers for practice
- How to discover thousands of "free" Spanish words that you already know, and how to learn strange new words quickly
- How even a basic Spanish vocabulary can help you understand a lot of Spanish
- More.

Conversational Spanish Made Easy
http://www.deepthoughtpress.com/converstaional-spanish

A carefully designed course that targets the most commonly used vocabulary and phrases in a number of common real-life situations.

- Over 80 lessons of conversational Spanish (4+ hours of video and PDF's).)
- Quizzes and Practice-Videos so you can test your listening and writing skills.
- Conversation Scenarios showcasing accents from 6 different Spanish-speaking countries.
- Direct access to your tutor for questions or to expand on any of the subjects.

Learn Spanish with Rosetta Stone
http://www.deepthoughtpress.com/rosetta-spanish

Develop your command of the language. From the simple to the complex, gain the confidence to share your ideas and opinions. Develop conversational skills to plan adventures, care for your health, and move abroad. Talk about government, work, movies, and citizenship. Discuss family and traditions, and celebrate success.

- Interactive language software with proprietary speech-recognition technology
- Develop your command of the language--read, write, speak, and understand
- Build vocabulary; negotiate complex situations; share ideas and opinions
- Enhance your learning on-the-go with Rosetta Stone mobile apps for the Kindle Fire HD, iPad and iPhone. Three month access included with purchase.
- The online games and lessons are only included for three months after which you must buy a subscription to continue using them.

Printed in Great Britain
by Amazon